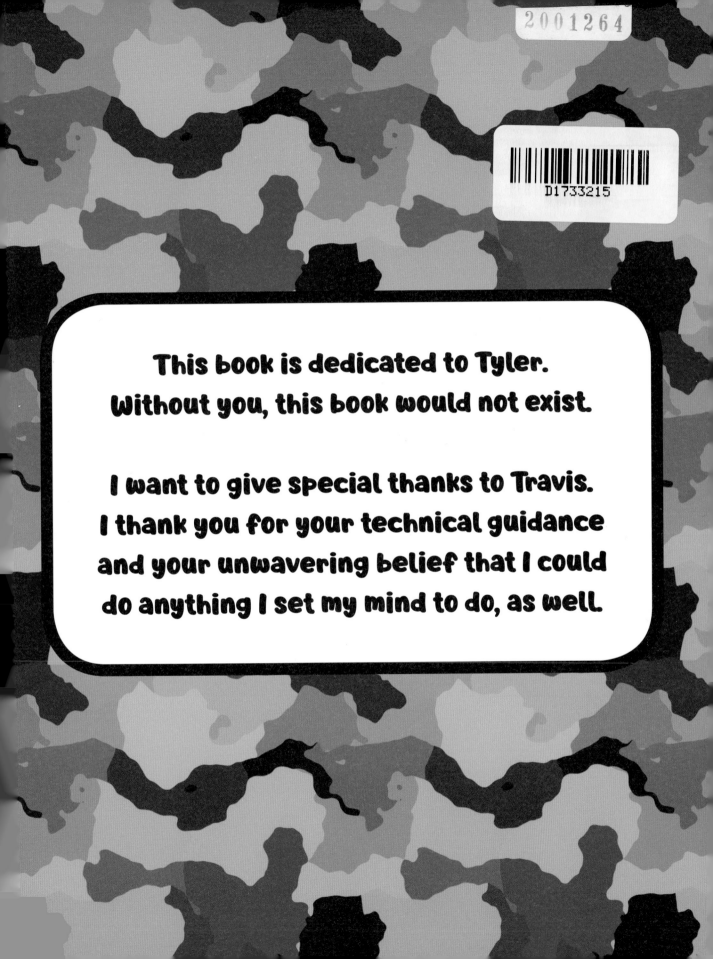

This book is dedicated to Tyler.
Without you, this book would not exist.

I want to give special thanks to Travis.
I thank you for your technical guidance
and your unwavering belief that I could
do anything I set my mind to do, as well.

www.mascotbooks.com

Who is Sam the Soldier?

©2019 Erin Morris. All Rights Reserved. No part of this publication may be reproduced, stored in a retrieval system or transmitted in any form by any means electronic, mechanical, or photocopying, recording or otherwise without the permission of the author.

For more information, please contact:
Mascot Books
620 Herndon Parkway, Suite 320
Herndon, VA 20170
info@mascotbooks.com

Library of Congress Control Number: 2019901919

CPSIA Code: PRT0519A
ISBN-13: 978-1-64307-563-1

Printed in the United States

Who is SAM the SOLDIER?

Erin Morris

illustrated by

Vipin Alex Jacob

This is Sam Smith.
He is a soldier in the
United States Army.

What is the Army? The United States Army is the oldest and largest branch of the armed forces.

The Army is responsible for protecting America and America's friends on the ground. The Army does its job using soldiers and large machines such as tanks and cannons. The Army is made up of soldiers from all over the world with different genders, religions, ethnicities, and races. The Army is very diverse.

Sam is a Private First Class in the Army, so the other soldiers call him Private Smith.

When Sam goes to work, he wears a uniform so everyone knows he is a soldier. Most of the time, he wears his utility uniform.

On special occasions, Sam wears his fancy uniform. It tells you all about Sam before you even meet him.

On the right side of Sam's uniform, you can see his last name. You can tell Sam's rank by looking at his sleeves. A soldier who has been in the Army for a long time and worked really hard will have a higher rank than a new soldier. Sam has been in the Army for two years and has earned the rank of Private First Class. If Sam keeps working hard, he can earn the rank of Specialist next.

You can also learn a lot about Sam by looking at the left side of his uniform. These are called ribbons. They represent different awards Sam has earned. Some of the ribbons tell you where Sam has been or that he has been well-behaved.

This ribbon represents the Army Achievement Medal. Sam earned that award for winning the Soldier of the Month competition.

Anytime you see a soldier in this uniform, you can always ask him or her what each ribbon represents.

There are many jobs in the Army. You can be in the infantry, where they use weapons.

You can be a medic and help people who are hurt.

You can be a pilot of a helicopter or a driver of a big truck.

You can be an artilleryman and work with cannons.

Sam is a mechanic, and he fixes big vehicles when they're broken.

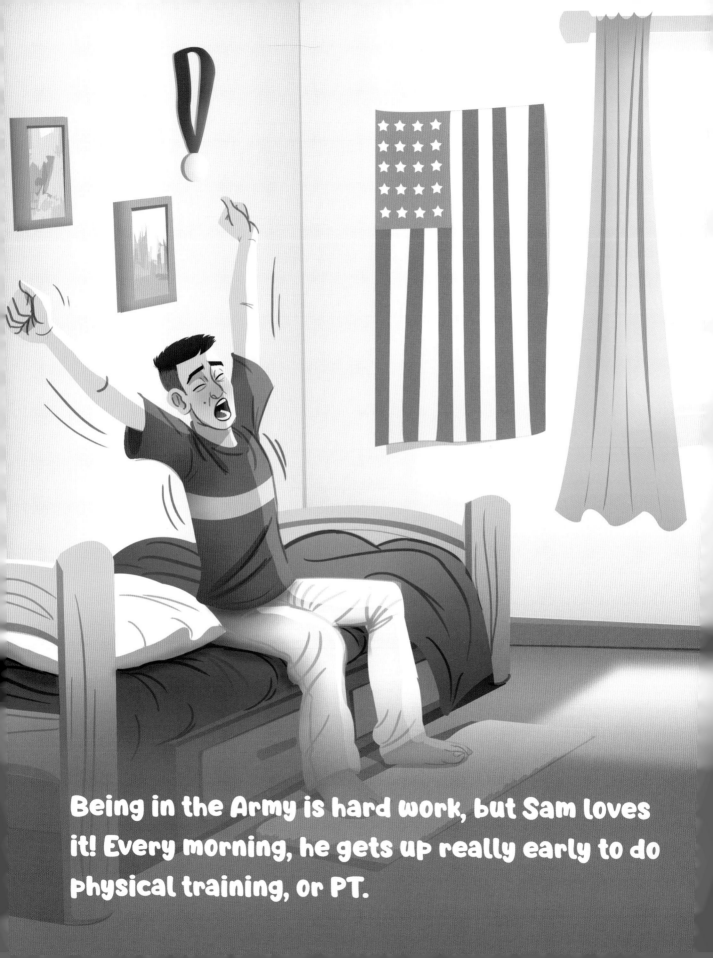

Being in the Army is hard work, but Sam loves it! Every morning, he gets up really early to do physical training, or PT.

His daily work always starts with exercise so the soldiers can stay healthy and strong.

Sam stands in formation with the rest of his company and salutes the flag before they get started.

Captain Bass and First Sergeant Franco
are Sam's bosses.

Sometimes, all of the companies in Sam's battalion get together and go for a battalion run.

That is Lieutenant Colonel Jensen and Command Sergeant Major Fisher. They are in charge of Sam's battalion.

After Sam exercises, he takes a shower and then goes to the dining facility, which the soldiers call the DFAC, to eat breakfast. Some of Sam's soldier friends cook and serve the other soldiers food here.

After breakfast, all of the soldiers get back to work.

When he finishes for the day, Sam goes back to his barracks room to prepare for the next day and hang out with his friends.

Sam likes being in the Army because he gets to serve his community and country and help people.

Sometimes, people need help because of natural disasters like hurricanes and floods. The soldiers help by bringing supplies, rescuing people, and providing first aid.

Sometimes, people in other countries are fighting and they need help. This is when soldiers have to go to war to defend America and America's friends from those who want to hurt or harm them. But that is only if they can't come to an agreement first. In the end, a soldier's job is to help keep everyone safe.

Sam is proud to be a soldier in the United States Army, and Sam's family is very proud of him, too.

ABOUT THE AUTHOR

Erin Morris is a former officer in the U.S. Army Judge Advocate General's Corps. She did one tour to Afghanistan with the 101st Airborne Division, where she discovered the true dedication and sacrifices of our nation's heroes. Erin is a proud supporter of the military and spends much of her free time supporting and serving veterans and veteran causes.

ABOUT THE ILLUSTRATOR

Even before he could remember, Vipin Alex Jacob has been passionate about drawing while communicating through it. For the past 11 years, Vipin has worked in several areas of children's entertainment, including designing for children's magazine publications, animation movie/TV series, toy designs, and children's books. Vipin currently resides with his family in Toronto, Canada. You can see more of his work on Instagram @vipin_alex_jacob or www.artstation.com/vipinjacob.